To all of the important organizations that do so much for literacy, especially Save the Children.
And to the Spectacular Six: Regan, Hale, and Cecilia Roberts, Jack, Cal, and Roland Hartman. No one could ask for more fun grandchildren.
—Cokie

For David and Peter,
Ever thine
—Diane

Ladies of Liberty. Text copyright © 2017 by Cokie Roberts. Illustrations copyright © 2017 by Diane Goode. All rights reserved. Manufactured in China.
No part of this book may be used or reproduced in any manner whatsoever without written permission except in the case of brief quotations embodied in critical articles and reviews.
For information address HarperCollins Children's Books, a division of HarperCollins Publishers, 195 Broadway, New York, NY 10007. www.harpercollinschildrens.com

ISBN 978-0-06-078005-0

The artist used pen, sepia ink, and Pan Pastels on Arches hot press watercolor paper to create the artwork for this book.

17 18 19 20 21 SCP 10 9 8 7 6 5 4 3 2 1   ❖ First Edition

COKIE ROBERTS

LADIES OF LIBERTY

The Women Who Shaped Our Nation

Illustrated by DIANE GOODE

HARPER

An Imprint of HarperCollinsPublishers

LETTER OF INTRODUCTION

*A*FTER AMERICA FOUGHT *the Revolution and formed a new nation, the really hard work began. It was easier for people from the different parts of the country to come together when they were fighting a common enemy— Great Britain. But once the original thirteen states were on their own, with a government to form and a country to run, the arguments started. One argument got settled pretty quickly: the question of where the nation's capital would be. A new city would be built on the banks of the Potomac River. It came to be called Washington, District of Columbia, and when the government moved there everyone was a newcomer. The politicians and their wives left family and friends to settle this strange new place, and some of them wrote lots of letters about the experience.*

That's one way we know about history, from letters. And women's letters are especially good at giving us the whole picture—not just what was happening in politics but also what the children were up to and what everyone was wearing: "her arms were uncovered," clucked Rosalie Calvert about a daring younger woman. The letters women wrote could be pretty funny in their remarks about the important men they knew as husbands and sons, fathers and friends, men we know as the Founding Fathers. "Mr. Madison was a very small man," according to John Quincy Adams's wife, Louisa, "with a very large head."

But we also learn about the past from the records people kept as they organized societies or opened schools. Women did much of that work. Mother Elizabeth Seton, for instance, started the parochial school system in America. Reform-minded women like Eliza Hamilton and Rebecca Gratz understood that even as the country was growing and many people were thriving, not everyone was doing well. So they protected widows and orphans, and they fed the hungry and found jobs for the needy. Happily for us, they recorded what they were doing, so we can learn about their activities more than two hundred years later.

Journals also teach a great deal about the women who came before us. Women who traveled west often kept diaries of their difficult journeys. Nineteen-year-old Margaret Dwight described one inn where she spent the night: "it serves for a tavern, a store & I should imagine hog's pen, stable & everything else." And the most famous journals, the ones kept by the explorers Lewis and Clark, introduce us to the remarkable Native American teenager Sacagawea, who greatly contributed to the success of the expedition across the continent.

And then there are the books written by the women of the time. Some were fun to read: bestselling novels like Hannah Foster's The Coquette. *Others like Hannah Crocker's* Observations on the Real Rights of Women *were less fun but still interesting because women were starting to discuss their proper place in this new country. These women were not allowed to vote. Married women could not own property. Even their clothes and jewelry belonged to their husbands. So women started thinking about their rights, while some of them also worked for the rights of the men and women trapped in the system of slavery.*

In this book you'll meet a few of the women who helped keep the brand-new United States together, working to make it a nation where everyone could pursue the happiness promised when America declared independence and proclaimed its freedom from tyranny. That's why I call them Ladies of Liberty.

Cokie Roberts

Women Through the Years

1727 The Ursuline nuns arrive in New Orleans from France and establish the first school for girls in America, which was also the first Catholic school in what would become the United States. They also teach African and Native Americans.

1746 A Native American raid on white settlers in Massachusetts inspires Lucy Terry Prince to compose the first African American poem, "The Bars Fight."

1790 Judith Sargent Murray's "On the Equality of the Sexes" starts people talking about women's rights.

1806 Eliza Hamilton works with Isabella Graham to form the Orphan Society Asylum in New York, which is still helping children today.

1809 James Madison becomes president, and Elizabeth Seton establishes the first American order of nuns, who run schools, hospitals, and orphanages.

1810 Margaret Dwight travels by wagon to Ohio as one of the women helping settle the West.

1814 The British invade Washington, frightening letter writers Sarah Seaton and Rosalie Calvert. But the American victory a few months later in New Orleans cheers Louise Livingston.

1797 Isabella Graham creates the Society for the Relief of Poor Widows with Small Children, and Hannah Foster publishes the bestselling novel *The Coquette*. Both aim to better women's position in society.

1799 Hannah Adams's New England history adds to her reputation as an author and helps make her the first woman in America to support herself by writing.

1801 Thomas Jefferson becomes president and makes friends with Margaret Bayard Smith, who writes about Washington for more than forty years. Jefferson's daughters come to visit the next year.

1805 Sacagawea helps Lewis and Clark on the expedition across the country to find out what Jefferson bought in the Louisiana Purchase in 1803.

1817 James Monroe becomes president after a career in politics, including ambassador to France. There his wife, Elizabeth, helps get Madame de Lafayette out of jail.

1818 Sacred Heart nun Philippine Duchesne opens the first free school west of the Mississippi River, Hannah Crocker publishes her views on the real rights of women, and Fanny Wright shocks the country.

1819 Rebecca Gratz starts a society for Jewish women, one of her several social service agencies, many of them aimed at helping fellow Jews.

1821 Emma Willard opens her academy for girls; Daughters of Africa do good works in Philadelphia, where Lucretia Mott also arrives to preach against slavery.

1825 John Quincy Adams becomes president after his wife, Louisa, works for his election. She has helped her husband succeed throughout his political and diplomatic careers.

LUCY TERRY PRINCE

"IN THIS REMARKABLE WOMAN THERE WAS AN ASSEMBLAGE OF qualities rarely to be found among her sex," one newspaper said about Lucy Prince after she died. It was unusual for newspapers to write about women at all in 1821. It was even more unusual for a woman who was a former slave. Brought from Africa when she was a tiny child, Lucy witnessed a raid by Native Americans on the white settlers of Deerfield, Massachusetts. Her verses about that event, called "The Bars Fight," make up the first known poem by an African American. Lucy recited the poem out loud instead of writing it down, and she became known as a "singer of history."

The poet married Abijah Prince, was freed from slavery, and moved to Vermont, where the couple raised six children. At least one of their sons fought in the Revolutionary War. Written records tell us those facts. Other stories about Lucy's speaking skills have been handed down

over the years. When her family's land had been illegally claimed by a neighbor, Lucy won it back in court, and some history books quote Supreme Court Justice Samuel Chase saying that Mrs. Prince "made a better argument than he had ever heard from a lawyer in Vermont."

In another often-told tale, Lucy tried to convince Williams College to accept her son as a student. Supposedly she talked to the men who ran the college for three straight hours, quoting many verses from the Bible, but they still rejected her son because he was black.

*H*ERE are some verses from "The Bars Fight":

Eunice Allen see the Indians coming

And hoped to save herself by running;

And had not her petticoats stopped her,

The awful creatures had not cotched her.

The words are spelled the way they were when the poem was published in 1855, more than one hundred years after Lucy first composed it. Before then, people spoke it aloud and memorized it.

Lucy Prince was a widow for twenty-seven years before her death at age ninety-seven. Every year until she died she traveled by horseback to visit her husband's grave. The newspaper story about her life said, "She was much respected among her acquaintance, who treated her with a degree of deference."

JUDITH SARGENT MURRAY

J. Sargent Murray

WHEN AMERICA BECAME A COUNTRY, THE MEN WHO DRAFTED the Declaration of Independence and the Constitution stressed the importance of liberty and self-rule, but they allowed only white men to vote and serve in the government—not women or African Americans. And married women could not own property. Even their clothes and jewelry belonged to their husbands. Some women wrote private letters, complaining about their second-class treatment, but one woman, Judith Sargent Murray, fought publicly for women's rights in her widely read magazine articles.

In one called "On the Equality of the Sexes," Judith asked if anyone thought a two-year-old boy was smarter than a two-year-old girl. She knew that the answer was no, and so she argued that women would be just as smart as men if girls could have the same education as boys. That was a shocking concept at the time because women were supposed to think about cooking and sewing and taking care of the family, not about books and ideas. Judith made the point that women could take care of the home *and* be educated so they could participate in government. She also wrote that an uneducated girl would be likely to marry the first man who "approaches her with tenders of love," even if he could not make her happy. Instead of the man being the boss, Judith believed that in a good marriage the husband and wife respected each other and were each other's friends. Many people read Judith's work and began to think more about equal rights for women.

AT FIRST Judith did not let people know that she was the author of her articles. She used the name "The Gleaner" to sign her work because she believed readers would take her writing more seriously if they thought it was by a man, even though it made her furious that "female productions" were often ignored. Articles by "The Gleaner" became very popular, so Judith kept her secret for a long time. Even her husband didn't know who "The Gleaner" was.

After a while Judith decided to publish all her articles together in a book with her own name as the author, not "The Gleaner." She wanted the credit for her work, expecting "a new era in female history." She asked President George Washington and Vice President John Adams to help her get the book published, and they did. Washington later told her that he read it with enjoyment.

ISABELLA GRAHAM

Bell Graham

Years after she created the Society for the Relief of Poor Widows with Small Children, Isabella Graham was able to claim: "Its fame is spread over the United States, and celebrated in foreign countries." It took a great deal of work to get to that point, and Isabella had to battle the men who laughed at her, saying that women could not "establish such an undertaking." But, along with other New York women, she bought a building, opened a school, and trained widows to teach children.

Isabella came up with all kinds of plans to get people out of poverty because she knew what it was like to be poor. When her husband died, leaving her with four children and pregnant with a fifth, she found that the money from his soldier's pension wasn't enough to live on. So she started girls' schools, first in Scotland and later in New York. The New York school became very popular; when Martha Washington was first lady, she sent her granddaughter Nelly there.

Isabella could see that there were many children who couldn't afford to go to school. The charity she organized soon provided food and clothes for about one hundred fifty widows, plus education for their more than four hundred children.

But if the mothers died, their children would often end up on the streets. To take care of them, Isabella and her friends created the Orphan Asylum Society and raised the money for an orphanage where the children could live and be trained for jobs. The society she started is still helping poor children in New York City today.

Sunday Schools

The Orphan Asylum Society

The Society For The Relief of Poor Widows With Small Children

ISABELLA became friends with a former slave named Catherine Ferguson who was a famous cake maker. "Katy" found homes for dozens of street kids and set up the School for the Poor. Sometimes the kids met at Isabella's house and sometimes at Catherine's. But then they moved to a church, and that's how Sunday schools started. They became an important way for poor children to get at least some education.

One of the ways we know so much about Isabella's work is that the societies she helped organize kept very good records. The first meeting of the Orphan Asylum Society took place on March 15, 1806, at the City Hotel on Broadway with "Mrs. Hamilton, widow of Gen. Alexander Hamilton," as one of the chief "promoters of the new organization." Eliza Hamilton, who had been left as a widow with seven children herself, stayed active in the orphanage organization for many years.

WOMEN EDUCATORS AND REFORMERS

THE AMERICAN IDEA THAT CITIZENS—or at least white male citizens—could elect their representatives was an experiment that hadn't been tried before. To make it work, government leaders thought the best way to raise good citizens would be to educate their mothers. Schools for girls started springing up, many of them run by women. Some of those women, plus a good many others, also saw problems with poverty in a young nation with no social welfare societies, so, often with a great deal of difficulty, they filled that need.

MOVING WEST

Another group of French nuns, led by Mother Rose Philippine Duchesne, arrived in Missouri in 1818. Though in the tiny town of St. Charles the only cooking oil was "bear grease and it is disgusting," it took Mother Duchesne just over a week to set up the first free school west of the Mississippi River. Eventually, Sacred Heart schools spread across America, and Philippine was named a saint.

IN THE BEGINNING . . .

The Ursuline nuns established the first school for girls in America, which was also the country's first Catholic school, in New Orleans in 1727. The sisters not only taught French colonists' daughters but they also started a free school for African and Native Americans. When Louisiana became part of the United States, President Jefferson told the nuns he would provide "all the protections which my office can give."

VOICE FOR THE VOICELESS

What they called "the sin of slavery" deeply concerned many American women. One of them, Lucretia Mott, made speeches against slavery and organized societies to call for the abolition of the horrible practice. Sometimes when she went to an anti-slavery meeting, she wasn't allowed to talk because she was a woman. So Mrs. Mott became a fighter for women's rights as well.

FIGHTER FOR FREEDOM

Some enslaved people were allowed to earn wages, which they saved to buy their freedom. Especially hard workers like Alethia Browning Tanner also helped others. She grew vegetables and sold them in Washington's central market and used her money to free many family members. The capital's African American community considered her a wise leader.

SELF-HELP SOCIETIES

In many cities, African American women organized to improve conditions in their communities. At St. Thomas's African Episcopal Church, Philadelphia women formed one of the earliest organizations. Soon women in Newport, Rhode Island, and Salem, Massachusetts, also created African aid societies to

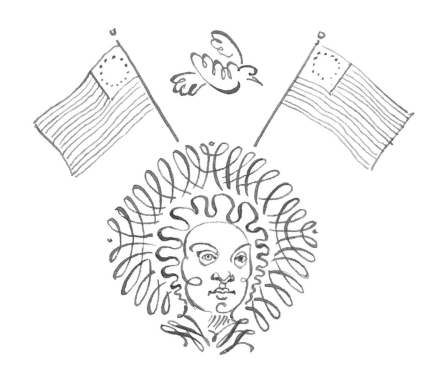

build schools and help those in need. Detailed records show that almost two hundred Daughters of Africa in Philadelphia pledged mutual assistance in 1821.

WEAVERS OF SAFETY NETS

Isabella Graham and Eliza Hamilton worked with women in New York to build an orphanage. They tirelessly raised money from the public, going to churches and staging benefits, and they convinced the state legislature to allocate five thousand dollars for the cause. Later in Washington, women saw a similar need to take care of fatherless children. First Ladies Dolley Madison and Louisa Adams both helped run the Orphan Asylum that eventually became Hillcrest Children's Center, which is still helping kids in the nation's capital.

SACAGAWEA

WHEN PRESIDENT THOMAS JEFFERSON BOUGHT THE Louisiana territory from France in 1803, he had no idea how big it was. So he sent Meriwether Lewis and William Clark to explore the vast land, and their journey led them all the way to the Pacific Ocean. The explorers knew that they would need to go by boat part of the way, but to complete the trip over the mountains they would need horses. The Shoshone Indians were famous for their horses, so the men were pleased when they found an interpreter—a man who could speak some Native American languages—with a Shoshone wife who would be able to negotiate with her tribe. Only a teenager at the time, Sacagawea, which means "Bird Woman," gave birth to a baby boy shortly before they set out on the long journey, with her carrying the baby on her back.

The men soon learned how important Sacagawea was because she

could find fruit and root vegetables they liked to eat. As they got closer to the Shoshone land, she was able to point the way. Once they found the Shoshones, Sacagawea realized that her brother had become chief, and she convinced him to exchange horses for guns and ammunition.

Though she was very happy to see her relatives again, she continued with the expedition to the Pacific and then helped guide it home. Captain Clark wrote that she was "of great service to me as a pilot" and that she "deserved a greater reward." Sacagawea received no reward at all after a year and half's journey, but later Clark helped educate her son.

Not long after the expedition began, a storm came up and swamped a boat with all of the provisions for the trip. Sacagawea, who Lewis said showed "equal fortitude" with the men, retrieved many of the items that had washed overboard and saved them. A few days later, the grateful men named a river in what is now Montana the Sacagawea River.

1804–1806 The Lewis and Clark Expedition

On the West Coast the explorers met some Native Americans they had never seen before. One was wearing an otter-skin robe "more beautiful than any fur I had ever seen," Clark wrote in his journal. The men tried to bargain for the fur, but the owner would not accept anything until he was offered Sacagawea's belt of blue beads. Poor "Bird Woman" had to give up a beautiful belt, and all she got in return was a blue cloth coat.

MARTHA JEFFERSON RANDOLPH

Randolph

THOMAS JEFFERSON'S WIFE HAD BEEN DEAD FOR MANY YEARS when he became president. He asked his friend Dolley Madison to help him with some of the entertaining, but he really wanted his married daughters to bring their children from Virginia and stay with him in the White House. When daughters Martha and Maria finally paid a visit, the town turned out to meet them, and one friend declared Maria "beautiful" with "winning manners" and Martha "rather homely" but "one of the most lovely women I have ever met."

Martha had been her father's close companion all her life. When her mother died, Maria was just a toddler. She stayed in America with an aunt when Jefferson became ambassador to France and brought Martha, called Patsy, with him to Paris. Some years later, a young slave woman named Sally Hemings brought Maria to France as well.

After they returned to Virginia, both Martha and Maria married their cousins. Martha quickly had six children. Maria had a hard time in childbirth, losing her first child at just a few days old. Her third baby's birth was so difficult that both Maria and the baby died. Only Martha was left to console her father and answer his pleas to come again to the White House, where her eighth child was born.

Once Jefferson left the presidency, Martha ran Monticello, her father's Virginia plantation. She had to feed all the people who came to visit and find rooms for them to sleep. One night fifty unexpected guests showed up!

$\mathcal{M}$ARTHA was just turning ten years old when her mother died, but she had to help her father because he was so sad. He didn't leave his room for three weeks, and she later wrote that she "was never a moment from his side." Then Thomas started riding his horse over the mountains, and his little girl went with him where she saw "many a burst of grief." Martha stayed devoted to her father for the rest of his life.

Martha gave birth to the first White House baby. The woman who was there taking care of her told a friend that after the baby was born she looked for some food for her patient, but she couldn't find any, "nor a servant in the house" to help her. "It was Bachelor Hall," she declared. The baby, James Madison Randolph, was Martha's eighth. She went on to have twelve children. Eleven of them lived to adulthood.

Elizabeth Bayley Seton

E A Seton

When Elizabeth Bayley was growing up in New York, she led a comfortable life as the daughter of a doctor. Then, at age nineteen, she married wealthy merchant William Seton. Life seemed perfect to the new bride: "My own home at 20 . . . ," she wrote. "All this and heaven too." Children soon followed, five of them in eight years, and the young mother worked with Isabella Graham and Eliza Hamilton helping poor widows and children. But everything changed after Elizabeth's husband lost both his business and his health.

With their daughter Anna Maria the couple sailed to Italy, hoping William would get well, but he died soon after they arrived. A kind Italian family, friends of William's from the banking business, took care of the widow and her eight-year-old, and Elizabeth decided to adopt the family's Catholic religion. Back in New York she opened a school to try to support her family, but she learned many people did not like Catholics and refused to send their children there. So Elizabeth moved to Baltimore, a city friendlier to Catholics, where she was invited by a French priest to open a girls' school.

There she also started the first American order of nuns, the Sisters of Charity, and accepted the gift of a house for them near the Maryland mountains. It was cold and they were hungry, but the women still managed to get a school going for the girls from the parish church, the first "parochial" school in the country. Elizabeth and the Sisters of Charity went on to open many schools, hospitals, and orphanages throughout the country. In 1975 the pope named her Saint Elizabeth Ann Seton, the first American-born saint.

Sisters of Charity ✝ Saint Elizabeth Ann Seton

WHEN Elizabeth and her husband and daughter first arrived in Italy, the police would not let them off
the ship because there had been a yellow fever epidemic in New York and the Italians were worried
the Americans would spread the disease. The family was sent to live in a *lazaretto*—a place where people with
infectious illnesses were kept. It was so cold that when Anna Maria found a piece of rope, she used it to play
jump rope to try to keep warm. By the time they could leave, William was so sick that he died.

When Elizabeth became a nun, she chose the clothes she was already wearing as a widow for the uniform, or
habit, that the sisters would wear. And she told the bishop in charge that, even though she was now a nun, her
children would come first; she would do what was right for them no matter what "other duties" she might have.

WOMEN WRITERS

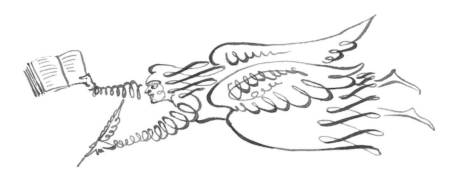

THE MAIN WAY WE LEARN the stories of people who lived long ago is through the written words they left behind. With no computers or telephones, letters were the means of communication. And thankfully some of those letters have been saved. Some people also kept diaries describing their daily lives, and others published books and articles that provide pictures of the times.

JOURNAL KEEPER

When nineteen-year-old Margaret Dwight journeyed from Connecticut to the Ohio frontier, she kept a journal showing how hard it was to travel by wagon—six weeks over rocky roads and staying in dirty inns. She had to get out and walk across the Allegheny Mountains to lighten the horses' load. All that exercise made her hungry and there wasn't much food for the travelers. But she made it to Ohio, soon married, and had thirteen children who helped settle what was then the West.

EDUCATIONAL ADVOCATE

Demanding better schools for women, Emma Willard sent her *Plan for Improving Female Education* to prominent men who liked her ideas. In 1821 the town of Troy, New York, agreed to help finance her girls' academy, which offered rigorous courses that attracted students from all over the country. Many graduates became teachers, spreading Emma Willard's educational ideas. Her school still educates young women.

NOVELIST

Hannah Foster's bestseller *The Coquette,* considered the first important novel by an American woman, was based on a true story. The central character had no money and was not trained to work, so she had to marry. But she didn't like either of the men who wanted to marry her, and she came to a sad end. The popular book showed that women needed to find ways to take care of themselves.

TWO MORE HANNAHS

Hannah Adams was the first American author to support herself by her writing. The success of her widely read histories made it easier for other women writers. One of them was Hannah Crocker, who in 1818 published her *Observations on the Real Rights of Women,* where she argued that women's judgment was "equal to the other sex."

REPORTERS

Margaret Bayard Smith arrived in Washington as a newspaperman's young bride just as the city became the nation's capital. In her letters she described the people and politics—Congressional debates were "attractive to the ladies"—and eventually started writing for newspapers, then added novels to her literary endeavors. Her family collected her letters for an important book: *The First Forty Years of Washington Society.*

During those years Scotswoman Fanny Wright amazed readers in the United States with her bold newspaper articles and brave speeches calling for women's equality and the abolition of slavery. She moved to America and helped publish the *Free Enquirer* newspaper in New York.

LETTER WRITERS

Rosalie Stier met and married George Calvert while her Belgian family lived in America. Once her relatives returned to Europe, she sadly never saw them again. But she was left in charge of her father's money and her letters describe how she invested it, along with the news of the growing United States and her fears for its future when the British invaded Washington in the War of 1812.

Also writing about that war was Sarah Gales Seaton, who, with her journalist husband, held a place at the center of political and social activity that she recounted in lively letters. When the war's hero, General Andrew Jackson, came to Washington, she wished "some little aerial machine" could be invented to bring her mother from North Carolina. Wouldn't she be surprised to see air travel today?

LOUISE D'AVEZAC LIVINGSTON

Louise Livingston

BORN IN HAITI ON THE ISLAND OF HISPANIOLA, LOUISE D'Avezac's family married her off to a much older man when she was only thirteen years old. While still a teenager she gave birth to three babies who died. Then her husband died, and a revolution on the island forced Louise to flee. After a dangerous boat trip, she and her little sister arrived in New Orleans, where most people spoke French, the language that Louise spoke.

The young refugees sold their jewelry for money to live on, and when they ran out of jewels, they started making clothes for other women. Though they worked hard, they had a good time at the many dinners and dances in the party-loving city. At one ball Louise met Edward Livingston, who had moved to New Orleans from New York. The couple fell in love and married, and the very beautiful and brilliant Louise became one of the most prominent women in the city.

When the British threatened New Orleans during the War of 1812, General Andrew Jackson arrived to defend the city. Louise thought he was a wild man from the woods of Tennessee and was upset when her husband invited Jackson to dinner. But she discovered that the general acted like a prince, and she liked him very much. She liked him even more when he led the Americans to a huge victory. After Jackson became president, he named Edward as his secretary of state and Louise moved with him to Washington, where she was very well respected because she was smart and interesting.

The Battle of New Orleans 1815

WHEN the Battle of New Orleans was over, Louise wrote to her sister-in-law: "I could not only hear the booming of the cannon, as the house shook each time, but every musket could be heard also." She added, "There never was a more glorious victory, nor one that cost less blood." The battle did not cost a great deal of American blood with only seventy-one casualties, but the British suffered a terrible loss with more than two thousand men dead, wounded, or missing.

Louise helped Edward with all his legal work. "I am never quite sure my decision is right until you have approved it," he wrote to her. She went with her husband to France when he became the American ambassador. After he died, she moved to his family estate in New York, where she became one of the country's first fighters for the environment.

REBECCA GRATZ

THE YOUNG AMERICAN NATION GREW QUICKLY BOTH IN SIZE AND population. And though many people found the country a wonderful place to make a good living, not everyone did. Some people, especially women and children, ended up living in poverty. Women all around the country saw the problems faced by poor people and worked to make their lives better. Rebecca Gratz, one of the most energetic and effective of those women, lived in Philadelphia, where she helped start several organizations aimed at improving the lives of the less fortunate. She especially helped others of her Jewish religion.

Rebecca grew up in a big, wealthy family—she was one of twelve children. Along with her mother and sister, she established the Female Association for the Relief of Women and Children in Reduced Circumstances. But she kept seeing more and more people in need, so she went on to help establish the Fuel Society, the Sewing Society, and then the Philadelphia Orphan Asylum. When she discovered that the children in the orphanage were taught Christianity, she worried that Jewish orphans were not learning about their faith. So Rebecca opened the first Jewish orphanage in America, taking children from all over the United States and Canada. She had studied Hebrew herself and joined with other women to create the first Hebrew Sunday school in the country, and her lesson plans were copied in other cities as Jewish education spread. When she died, the newspapers called her "a lady of singular accomplishments."

THOUGH Rebecca was incredibly busy running all the organizations she helped set up, she also had to take care of her family. She never married, but when her sister Rachel died leaving six children, they became Rebecca's "constant and tenderest concern" after they moved in with her and her brothers.

There's a romantic story about Rebecca that was in all the newspapers after she died. She was friendly with many of the famous artists and writers of her time, and one of those writers went to England, where he met Sir Walter Scott. When Scott's popular novel *Ivanhoe* told the tale of a Jewish woman named Rebecca and her doomed love of the Christian Ivanhoe, everyone assumed that the character was based on the very beautiful Rebecca Gratz, who had never married, something highly unusual for a woman at that time.

Elizabeth Kortright Monroe

Elizabeth Monroe.

When a friend of the young politician James Monroe saw Elizabeth Kortright and her sisters at the theater in New York, he wrote that they "made so brilliant and lovely an appearance" that other theatergoers flocked around them. James got the message and soon wooed and won the seventeen-year-old beauty. A few years after they were married, President George Washington named Monroe the American ambassador to France, and the couple headed to Paris with their seven-year-old daughter, Eliza.

It was a hard time to be there because France was in the middle of a revolution, but Elizabeth charmed the Parisians who called her *la belle Américaine*, "the beautiful American." When they went home to Virginia, James was elected governor. Then his friend Thomas Jefferson became president and sent the couple back to France, this time with a new baby girl, Maria, along with sixteen-year-old Eliza. Back again in America, James was named secretary of state to President James Madison, putting him in a good position to become president himself. Letters from the time describe Elizabeth as "charming and very beautiful," but she was sick much of the time, and her daughter Eliza filled in as First Lady. Many people in Washington found Eliza difficult to deal with because she could be rude and haughty.

The White House had been burned by the British in the War of 1812, and the Monroes stayed in their own house until they could repair and furnish the president's mansion. Some of the furniture that James and Elizabeth bought is in the White House today.

DURING the French Revolution, the wife of the American Revolutionary hero Marquis de Lafayette was thrown in jail. The United States wanted her released but couldn't officially deal with the French government, which was in turmoil. So Elizabeth Monroe bravely rode to the prison in the carriage of the American minister and asked to see Madame de Lafayette. James Monroe later wrote that news of his wife's visit "spread through Paris and had the happiest effect." Seeing the interest of the Americans in Lafayette's wife's case, the French government set her free.

The Monroes hosted the first White House wedding. Their seventeen-year-old daughter, Maria Hester, married the president's secretary, Samuel Gouverneur, who was also her cousin. Maria's much older sister, Eliza, took charge of the event and insisted that only forty-two people be invited. Women in Washington were furious because they had been looking forward to seeing young Maria married.

LOUISA CATHERINE ADAMS

Louisa Catherine Adams

LOUISA CATHERINE JOHNSON WAS LIVING IN LONDON WITH HER parents, six sisters, and a brother when young John Quincy Adams started dropping by for dinner. Eventually, he asked Louisa to marry him, but then he left to help represent America in Holland. He told his fiancée that he had no idea when he would be back, but while he was gone he wanted her to study some books he gave her. She didn't think that was very romantic.

After the couple married they moved to Berlin, where the king and queen paid a great deal of attention to them because John's father, John Adams, had been elected president of the United States. But President Jefferson had taken office by the time Louisa made her first trip to America in 1801, so her in-laws weren't in Washington when she moved there with her husband and little boys for John's job as a senator. Then it was back to Europe, this time as ambassador to Russia, and Louisa was very sad that her two older boys stayed in Boston with their grandparents and that only baby Charles traveled with her and John.

The king of

Russia—called the tsar—liked Louisa very much, inviting her to enormous balls at the palace. John's next job took the family back to London, where their older boys joined them, making their mother very happy. Home in America again, John became secretary of state and Louisa started throwing huge parties, trying to convince her hundreds of guests to help elect her husband president. It worked. Louisa Adams became First Lady, just like her mother-in-law, Abigail Adams.

In Russia, Louisa was surprised to learn that even children were expected at fancy balls just for them. At the first, she dressed two-year-old Charles as a Native American chief, and the other mothers applauded when he marched in. Louisa wrote home in amazement that the toddlers danced and then had an "elegant supper" with "oceans of champagne for the little people."

When his tour as ambassador was over, John Quincy went to Paris and sent word for Louisa to meet him there. That meant traveling with a seven-year-old across Europe in the dark of winter. It was a terrifying journey—the carriage broke down and the men traveling with them took off because war was breaking out. Soldiers, seeing her Russian carriage, threatened to attack, but Louisa used her wits and her excellent French to make it to Paris after forty harrowing days. Her husband simply wrote in his diary that "she and Charles are both well."

$\mathscr{C}$onclusion

At a time of tremendous change with the country expanding and experimenting, women were in the middle of it all. As new frontiers opened, American families moved to settle the uncharted lands. The wagon ride to unknown territory could be terrifying, but women courageously caravanned west, leaving friends and family behind, creating community out of the wilderness. And those brave women were just some of the many who used their time and their talents to make this country a better place for everyone.

Reformers and religious organizers, writers and teachers, explorers and settlers, political advisers and diplomatic helpmates—they all contributed to shaping our nation. And they did it with pluck and prayer, with fun and fortitude, with humor and heroics. The Constitution was a new document at the time of these Ladies of Liberty, but they knew that it aimed to form "a more perfect union." And they set about doing just that—toiling to make America a more perfect place for all of its people.

Acknowledgments

Diane Goode has once again created a collection of crisp and charming images of the women who made such a difference in the early years of our Republic. Having witnessed what an incredible impact her illustrations for our earlier book, *Founding Mothers*, had on our young readers, I was eager to see what her incredibly talented pen would produce for this book. What a treat it has been to watch the personalities of these women emerge through Diane's drawings. A huge thank-you to her.

And another one to our editor, Alyson Day. Alyson waded into the "grown-up" version of this book and culled the characters who would be interesting for youngsters—something I would have had a very difficult time doing on my own. She's not only a patient and practiced guide, Alyson's an enthusiastic cheerleader for both of these history books. Also at HarperCollins: art supervisor Rachel Zegar, copy editor Alexei Esikoff, senior marketing director Matt Schweitzer, senior marketing manager Katie Fee, and senior publicist Olivia Russo. And thank you too to DeeDee DeBartlo, who has made sure that the public knows about all of my books.

None of those books would exist without Claire Wachtel, my dear friend and editor. Another dear friend, Ann Charnley, helped me with much of the research for the "grown-up" book with assistance from the Massachusetts, Virginia, New York, Washington, and South Carolina Historical Societies, the University of South Carolina, the Jefferson and Huntington Libraries, Historic Hudson Valley, Monticello, Mount Vernon, the Dolley Madison Digital Edition, the American Antiquarian Society, the New York and Boston Public Libraries, and the Library of Congress, plus the members of the extended Livingston family. In addition, for this book, Diane's quest to find as many of the women's signatures as possible was aided by AnnaLee Pauls at Princeton University, who found Louise Livingston for us; and our search for the product of Isabella Graham's own pen led us first to Sandra April at Graham-Windham, the successor organization to Mrs. Graham's Orphan Asylum, who in turn sent us to the New-York Historical Society, where my friend Dale Gregory put us in touch with Eleanor Gillers, who found what we were after. A thanks to all.

Finally, big thank-yous to Bob Barnett, my friend and lawyer par excellence; to Kim Roellig, who keeps everything clicking in my life; and to my wonderful family, especially my husband, Steven, and our dog, Ella.

Cokie Roberts

Just as *Founding Mothers* was a labor of love, with many working to bring it to life, so too was *Ladies of Liberty*. When the subject is extraordinary women, we all step up to honor them.

I want to thank another extraordinary woman, Cokie Roberts, who was never more than a click away no matter where she was in the world and who made me laugh. I also want to thank my agent, Steve Malk at Writers House, for putting us together, and our talented designer, Rachel Zegar, who hung in there during those final twelve-hour workdays that stretched out into weeks as hundreds of scans flew back and forth. I'm grateful for our editor, Alyson Day, for allowing me a free hand and who gave me a hand when I needed it. And, of course, I'm thankful for the love and support of my husband, David, who has seen me through a lifetime of illustrating books.